My First Animal Library

Wolves

by Cari Meister

Bullfrog
Books

Ideas for Parents and Teachers

Bullfrog Books let children practice reading informational text at the earliest reading levels. Repetition, familiar words, and photo labels support early readers.

Before Reading

- Discuss the cover photo. What does it tell them?

- Look at the picture glossary together. Read and discuss the words.

Read the Book

- "Walk" through the book and look at the photos. Let the child ask questions. Point out the photo labels.

- Read the book to the child, or have him or her read independently.

After Reading

- Prompt the child to think more. Ask: Have you seen or heard a wolf? Where did you see him or her?

Bullfrog Books are published by Jump!
5357 Penn Avenue South
Minneapolis, MN 55419
www.jumplibrary.com

Library of Congress Cataloging-in-Publication Data

Meister, Cari, author.
 Wolves / by Cari Meister.
    pages cm. — (Bullfrog books.
My first animal library)
 Audience: Age 5.
 Audience: K to grade 3.
 Includes index.
 ISBN 978-1-62031-170-7 (hardcover) —
 ISBN 978-1-62496-257-8 (ebook)
 1. Wolves—Juvenile literature. I. Title.
QL737.C22M444 2015
599.773—dc23

2014032136

Series Editor: Wendy Dieker
Series Designer: Ellen Huber
Book Designer: Michelle Sonnek
Photo Researcher: Michelle Sonnek

All photos by Shutterstock except: Animals Animals, 21, 23br; biosphoto, 14, 18–19; Juniors Bildarchiv, 20–21; Nature Picture Library, 16–17; SuperStock, 5; Thinkstock, cover, 3, 6, 9, 10–11, 23tl, 23bl.

Printed in the United States of America at Corporate Graphics in North Mankato, Minnesota.

Table of Contents

A Hunt

A wolf puts his nose in the air.

He sniffs.

Wolves have a good sense of smell.

The wolf smells a deer.

Ah-WOOO!

The wolf howls.
He calls his pack.

He is the alpha wolf.

He is in charge.

It is time to hunt!

alpha

The pack runs.

They have long legs.

They run in deep snow.

The pack finds the deer.

They fight.

The deer kicks.

The pack wins.

It is time to eat.

The alpha eats first.
The hunters eat next.

There is meat left.
The pack brings it home.
Now the pups eat.
Yum!

pups

21

Parts of a Wolf

fur
Thick fur helps keep wolves warm in winter.

teeth
Wolves show their sharp teeth to warn away other wolves.

legs
Long, strong legs help wolves run for a long time without getting tired.

Picture Glossary

alpha
The leader of a pack of wolves.

pack
A group of wolves that lives and hunts together.

howl
One of the sounds a wolf makes; howling helps bring a pack together before a hunt.

pups
Baby wolves.

Index

To Learn More

Learning more is as easy as 1, 2, 3.

1) Go to www.factsurfer.com

2) Enter "wolves" into the search box.

3) Click the "Surf" button to see a list of websites.

With factsurfer.com, finding more information is just a click away.